CHURCHILL
AND
CHARTWELL

ROBIN FEDDEN

D0880450

PERGAMON PRESS

© 1968 Robin Fedden

Printed in Great Britain by
Westerham Press Ltd, Westerham, Kent
for the publishers
Pergamon Press Ltd, Oxford

First edition 1968
Reprinted 1972 and 1974 (with corrections)

08 013053 4

Contents

Foreword

BY BARONESS SPENCER-CHURCHILL

MY husband and I lived at Chartwell for over forty years. The written word cannot describe all that it meant to us, and to our children who grew up there. None the less, this guidebook sympathetically evokes the atmosphere of the house we loved and the garden that we made. Those who did not know Chartwell in our time will find much of my husband and of the house itself in these pages.

Preface

No true account of Chartwell could be written without the co-operation of Sir Winston's family. I owe much to the help given me by Lady Churchill, the late Randolph Churchill, and Lady Soames. I owe hardly less to Miss Hamblin, who was secretary at Chartwell for thirty-three years.

I also want to record the debt which the National Trust and every visitor to Chartwell owe to Lady Churchill. But for her generosity and public spirit the house would have come to the Trust as an empty shell. She not only ensured that most of the contents, things with which she had lived for many years and to which she was deeply attached, should be acquired by the Treasury in payment of death duty for retention at Chartwell, but she gave many of her own possessions so that the character of the house might remain unchanged. It is directly due to her initiative that Chartwell is so fascinating and personal a memorial to her husband.

Again it was only with the help of Lady Churchill and Lady Soames that the Trust was able to put back the clock, and so restore to certain rooms their appearance in the years before the war, when Chartwell – the house of a man out of office and out of favour – was paradoxically the most important country house in Europe.

Footnotes would be out of place in this guide. Passages in quotation come either from Churchill's books and speeches or from the following publications: Jean Améry, *Churchill*, 1965; Earl of Birkenhead, *The Prof. in Two World Wars*, 1961; Violet Bonham-Carter, *Winston Churchill as I knew him*, 1965; Randolph Churchill, *Winston S. Churchill*, vols. 1 and 2, 1966 and 1967; *Winston Spencer Churchill*, 1954; Sarah Churchill, *A Thread in the Tapestry*, 1967; Virginia Cowles, *Winston Churchill*, 1953; Dwight D. Eisenhower, *Crusade in Europe*, 1949; Christopher Hassell, *Edward Marsh*, 1959; Norman MacGowan, *My Years with Churchill*,

1958; Anthony Montague Browne, 'Chartwell', *Illustrated London News*, 1967; Lord Moran, *Winston Churchill*, 1966; Earl of Oxford and Asquith, *Memories and Reflections*, 1928; Gerald Pawle, *The War and Colonel Warden*, 1963; Philip Tilden, *True Remembrances*, 1954.

The quotation on p. 47 from the Churchill papers is reproduced by permission.

1974   R.F.

Dates

1874 Churchill born at Blenheim, November 30th.
1893 enters the Army
1898 at battle of Khartoum with Nile Expeditionary Force
1899 *Morning Post* correspondent in South Africa; escapes after capture by the Boers
1900 elected Member for Oldham
1906 Under-Secretary of State for the Colonies; publication of *Lord Randolph Churchill*
1908 President of the Board of Trade; marries Clementine Hozier
1910 Home Secretary
1911 First Lord of the Admiralty
1917 Minister of Munitions
1919 Secretary of State for War and Air
1922 out of office and the House of Commons; buys Chartwell
1923 publication of *The World Crisis*
1924 re-enters House of Commons as Member for Epping; appointed Chancellor of the Exchequer; moves into Chartwell
1929 out of office for a decade and lives mainly at Chartwell
1933 publication of *Marlborough*
1939 First Lord of the Admiralty
1940 Prime Minister and Minister of Defence
1945 electoral defeat of the Tory party
1947 first exhibits at the Royal Academy
1949 publication of *The Second World War*
1951 Prime Minister for the second time
1953 receives Order of the Garter
1955 resigns office in April
1963 created Honorary Citizen of the United States
1965 dies on January 24th, nearly two months after his ninetieth birthday.

1. The Background

WINSTON CHURCHILL moved with his family to Chartwell in 1924. Except during the war, it was to be his home for forty years. These pages attempt to relate the man to the place. Biographical only in a limited sense, they trace Churchill's relationship with a house and its contents, and with a garden. The events of his career are seen obliquely, as they emerge from Chartwell or reflect upon it.

In 1922 when Churchill bought the house he was nearly forty-eight. With a brilliant if chequered career behind him, he resigned as Secretary of State for the Colonies in October 1922, after working for a sensible settlement in a chaotic Middle East and for reconciliation in a faction-ridden Ireland. A few weeks before Chartwell became his, and at a time when his loyalty to the Liberal party was under strain, Lloyd George's coalition fell. Churchill found himself out of office and for the first time since 1900 without a seat in parliament. He was, following an operation for appendicitis and his rejection by the Dundee electors, 'without an office, without a seat, without a party, and without an appendix'. Only the loss of the appendix was permanent. In the same year that he moved into Chartwell, he was, after fighting three unsuccessful elections, back in parliament as 'Constitutionalist' member for Epping, and in office in Baldwin's government as Chancellor of the Exchequer. Most of the first Chartwell period (1922-9) was thus one of activity as a minister. It must be seen in the context of his five budgets, his return to the gold standard, and of such events as Locarno, the General Strike of 1926, and the Anglo-French naval pact of 1928.

At Chartwell it is no less important to see these years, even more than later periods, in terms of family life. Chartwell was a home, and an unusually happy one, in which children were growing up. Churchill married his wife, Clementine Hozier, whom he always called 'Clemmie', some months after his success in the general election of 1908. He was thirty-four and she was twenty-two. Her father was Colonel Sir Henry Hozier, and her mother a daughter of the Earl of Airlie. It was an outstandingly successful marriage. As Churchill wrote later, 'I married and lived happily ever afterwards.' Others must have been reminded of his married life on reading the words he wrote about the marriage of John and Sarah Churchill, his illustrious ancestors: 'The facts could not be disputed. They proclaim the glory of that wedlock in which the vast majority of civilised mankind find happiness and salvation in a precarious world.' Lady Churchill for over half a century was his close partner in adversity and in triumph. Her loyalty was proverbial. To envisage Churchill at Chartwell is also to think of Lady Churchill, and not least in terms of her genius for organisation. Churchill's home was run with perfect efficiency. In recognition of long public service, which began with the establishment of canteens for munition workers in the First World War, Lady Churchill received the G.B.E. in 1946 and was created a life peeress in 1965 shortly after her husband's death, taking the title of Baroness Spencer-Churchill of Chartwell.

When the Churchills moved into Chartwell their son Randolph was thirteen, their two elder daughters Diana and Sarah were fifteen and ten, and their youngest daughter Mary only two. It was thus a house of nurseries and nursemaids. For his children Churchill found time to build a two-storey 'house' high in the branches of a lime tree and a miniature cottage in the walled garden. Much at Chartwell recalls both his children and his grandchildren.

His son Randolph was to prove a controversial figure. Highly independent, he shared many of his father's qualities of temperament and character. He was thus well-fitted for the role of official biographer. Two impressive volumes of his authoritative work on Churchill appeared before his death. During the war Randolph Churchill was commissioned in his father's old regiment, the 4th Hussars, and served in the Western Desert, Italy and Yugoslavia. At the same time (1940–5) he sat in parliament as M.P. for Preston. Subsequently he unsuccessfully contested several elections, where ironically the fact that he was his father's son proved a serious disadvantage. The energy that was barred an outlet in politics, and an inherited gift for words, subsequently made him one of the most powerful journalists of his time. His son Winston is now M.P. for Stretford.

Two of Churchill's daughters married politicians. The eldest,

8

Diana, married Duncan Sandys. He entered parliament in 1935, holding Ministerial office from 1944 to 1945 and again uninterruptedly from 1951 to 1964 in a number of important posts which included Defence, Aviation, and the Colonies. In 1947 he started the European Movement and nine years later was inspired to found the Civic Trust. The youngest daughter, Mary, married Christopher Soames. He entered parliament in 1950 and during his father-in-law's last term of office as prime minister was his parliamentary private secretary. Subsequently, after holding junior office at the Air Ministry and the Admiralty, he was Secretary of State for War (1958–60), Minister of Agriculture (1960–64), and Ambassador in Paris (1968–72). In 1973 he was appointed Commissioner of External Relations in Brussels. Churchill's third daughter Sarah, now the widow of the twenty-third Lord Audley, made a career on the stage. She is almost equally talented as a painter and writer. Several of her drawings hang at Chartwell and her book *A Thread in the Tapestry* evokes her close relations with her father.

In 1929 the background of life at Chartwell changed dramatically and not for the last time. Baldwin's Government fell and Labour was returned with Liberal support. Churchill was out of office for ten years. Neither the Coalition Government when it came in 1931, nor Baldwin's second administration in 1935, had room for him. His ideas were not those of this indeterminate decade. He was in a political desert. In this desert Chartwell was his oasis.

'I lived mainly at Chartwell', he says, speaking of these years, 'where I had much to amuse me. I built with my own hands a large part of the cottages and extensive kitchen-garden walls, and made all kinds of rockeries and waterworks and a large swimming pool which was filtered to limpidity and could be heated to supplement our fickle sunshine. Thus I never had a dull or idle moment from morning to midnight, and with my happy family around me dwelt at peace within my habitation.' In somewhat the same vein he wrote in 1932 to his ailing friend Edward Marsh, who had first become his parliamentary secretary nearly thirty years earlier, inviting him to Chartwell, 'You could rest comfortably here . . .', he said, 'Just vegetate as I do.'

This picture of the statesman in tranquil and bucolic retirement, a latter-day Cincinnatus busied with his garden, is attractive but misleading. If Chartwell was an oasis, it was also a hive of activity. Walls, waterworks, and the painting of pictures were the relaxations of an assiduous member of parliament, the diversions of a busy historian. In these years at Westminster he offered provocation impartially to Ramsay Macdonald's supporters and to Baldwin's Conservatives, and wrote at Chartwell the four volumes of his definitive biography of Marlborough. It was hardly vegetation.

To Chartwell in September 1931 his friend Brendan Bracken brought news of the imminent departure from the gold standard, which Churchill had restored as Chancellor of the Exchequer, and to Chartwell soon after began to come information from Germany of a more ominous sort. With a historian's grasp of the sweep of events Churchill saw and feared the implications of Hitler's rise to power. A shadow fell over the house and garden. As the thirties took their dire course, he turned to fight the menace that threatened Europe. Almost alone he foresaw the wrath to come and tried to awake his countrymen to the dangers ahead. His solitary campaign in these years has been described, and perhaps rightly, as 'without parallel in English history'. In parliament, and for long to little effect, he alternately thundered or patiently offered statistics which should have convinced. At Chartwell he developed his own intelligence service. It has been called at this time 'a little Foreign Office'. A stream of visitors brought the information, the facts and figures, which provided the ammunition for his campaign. It was the hub of resistance. Slowly the number of his adherents increased. Too slowly, for in the summer of 1939 the storm broke. Churchill was again summoned to office, and Chartwell for five years retired from history.

The lakes at Chartwell made the place easily identifiable from the air by enemy planes – as a protective measure they were strewn with brushwood – and when the invasion of the Kent coast seemed imminent this was no place for a prime minister. Chartwell was closed for the war, and when Churchill went to the country it was to Chequers or to Mr Ronald Tree's house in Oxfordshire, Ditchley Park. Yet he could not bear separation from Chartwell. Before the war he had built a cottage across the garden adjoining his studio, and here he contrived rare visits, sometimes coming down briefly from London to think and relax. He came alone in 1941 to await news of General Wavell's attack on Rommel's army in the Western Desert. When he learnt of its failure he paced the park for long hours. Two years later, when he had escaped for a night to the cottage, Maisky, the Russian Ambassador, arrived on

VIEW OF CHARTWELL

Courtesy of 'Country Life'

a perturbed visit. But the war years only play a marginal part in the story of Chartwell.

By the end of 1945 the house had been reopened and Churchill was back. He was also out of office, and was to remain so for nearly six years. His fall from power in July that year, a sudden slap in the face from the country he had saved, would have floored lesser men. As in 1929, he found solace at Chartwell. 'Winston is happy at Chartwell', an observer wrote, 'as happy as he can be when the world has gone all wrong.' Once again his family life, and the house and valley to which he was attached, were a source of strength. Once again, though he was now some fifteen years older, they were the base from which he exercised an intense activity. In his first eclipse he had written the life of Marlborough; now he applied himself to the history of the Second World War.

Though the post-war response was equally vigorous, there were clearly great differences between 1929 and 1945. Churchill was now the most respected man in Europe, the leader of the Opposition and of the very party which had once tried to break him. Chartwell was not an oasis, but a shrine. For the world it had changed. A small country house in Kent had developed an aura. It was no longer merely a family home. Visitors came to pay homage at the gates of a house that had become a fragment of history.

In 1951 the Conservatives regained office and Chartwell was once more the home of a prime minister. Churchill was almost seventy-seven. No man had spared himself less, or led a fuller and more active life. The end of so strenuous a career could only be a matter of time. He retired as prime minister a few months after his eightieth birthday. It was inevitably to Chartwell that he went. 'I love the place', he said and announced the intention of burying himself in the country. For such a man, even in old age and in the peace of Chartwell, inactivity was impossible. He continued to write and paint, and the things which had originally drawn him to Chartwell – the green valley and the views – lost nothing of their appeal. He walked daily in the garden, though with less certain step, or would sit looking at his roses, sheltered from the wind by the walls he had built nearly forty years earlier. Yet as time wore on he became more silent. The voice which had spoken so much to such purpose was gradually stilled. In his daughter's phrase he was waiting 'with increasing patience and courtesy for the end'. He would often ask the time. 'Noble spirits', as he said of Marlborough, 'yield themselves willingly to the successively falling shades which carry them to a better world or oblivion'. Shortly before his ninetieth birthday he left Chartwell for the last time. No other place had meant as much to him.

2. A House Transformed

A FEW miles north of Penshurst a combe climbs to the timbered summit of the Kent hills. Its suave green slopes evoke a sense of pastoral and, somewhere about the 600-foot contour, it is flanked by sheltering woods. Fertile soil overlays the local ragstone, and the trees, mainly chestnut, beech and oak, grow to great size. Their shadows at dawn and sunset are thrown far across the combe. Southward the view stretches to the Weald. On one side of this little valley rises a clear spring, the Chart Well, from which its name derives. Wooded, watered, smoothly pastured, this place must have commended itself to the eye and spirit since the Kentish landscape was first tamed.

The earliest recorded owner, about 1350, was William At-Well, so called from the spring which rose on his property. From the second half of the fourteenth century until the reign of James I the property belonged to a family named Potter from whom it passed by marriage to Sir John Rivers, Bt. The latter about the time of the Restoration conveyed it to Thomas Smith, described by Hasted, the Kentish historian, as a scrivener of London. For most of the eighteenth century it was in the ownership of the Ellisons. After passing through several hands, it was bought in 1848 by John Campbell Colquhoun, and remained in his family until its sale in 1922.

In the eighteenth century the road which passes the house was appropriately known as Well Street and a small hamlet of the same name was situated near the top of the hill. The site of the present building was occupied by a farmhouse. It was modest enough until enlarged as a Victorian country mansion by John Campbell Colquhoun soon after the middle of the nineteenth century.

In July 1921 the Chartwell estate, something over 800 acres, was offered for sale by auction. The house and nearly eighty acres which included the park, the uppermost reach of the Chart combe and its

13

fringing woods, did not reach the reserve of £6,500. Churchill bought it in November of the following year for £5,000. *The World Crisis*, his book on the First World War, is sometimes said to have provided the money. This seems improbable. The first of the four volumes was not published until 1923. More relevant is the fact that in 1921 Churchill had inherited a considerable sum on the death of a relative, Lord Herbert Vane-Tempest.

Chartwell was a bargain even in terms of the solid pounds of the time – the standing timber alone was valued at nearly £2,000 – but it was a buy prompted by enchantment. The new owner's feeling for landscape, which finds expression in his paintings, was responsible. He had been captivated by a combe and its setting. Many years later, looking out across the Weald, he said, 'I bought Chartwell for that view.' Providentially the view was also within twenty-five miles of Westminster. Given subsequent events, it is a curious coincidence that the National Trust, as the owners of Toy's Hill and Crockham Hill near by, considered buying Chartwell before the auction but were unable to find the money.

In the autumn of 1922 Churchill with his daughters Diana and Sarah and his son Randolph drove down to Chartwell. On the way he told them they were going to inspect a house he was thinking of buying. 'Do you like it?' he said when they arrived. The children were enthusiastic. Only on their return, as they drove across Parliament Square, did he announce the secret that Chartwell was already theirs.

Though its air of romantic desertion appealed to the children, in 1922 the house itself had little to commend it. Contemporary photographs show an ungainly Victorian mansion, ponderous with bays and oriels, its façade shrouded in ivy and its approach heavy with laurel, rhododendron, and conifer. It was dark and infested with dry rot. But the position, as Churchill appreciated, was splendid; set on a hillside, its differing levels provided drama. He saw its possibilities and at once set about rebuilding. The transformation of Chartwell cost close on £18,000.

He was to have time to devote to the problem. The Coalition Government fell in October 1922 and Churchill, after the general election, was not only out of office but out of the House of Commons for the first time since 1900. The better to supervise operations he took a lease of Hosey Rigge, a roomy house near by with a literary association

CHARTWELL IN 1922

CHARTWELL TO-DAY

that must have pleased him. Lewis Carroll had lived there when writing *Alice in Wonderland*. His architect at Chartwell was Philip Tilden, who enjoyed at the time considerable patronage. He seems first to have met Churchill at Sir Philip Sassoon's house in Kent, Port Lympne, to which he had made additions. But the choice of architect may have been influenced by the fact that Tilden was an old friend of Churchill's favourite aunt, Lady Leslie, and that in the previous year he had begun building a country house at Churt for his friend Lloyd George. Though Tilden is said to have been a reluctant architect, pushed and prodded by Lady Churchill, he clearly enjoyed his commission and the creation of an airy house 'out of the drabness of Victorian umbrageousness'. 'No client that I have had', he wrote thirty years later, ' . . . has ever spent more time, trouble, or interest in the making of his home.' As in all else, the client was thorough.

The entrance front as transformed by Churchill and his architect lost its ivy and many of its Victorian trimmings. It was simplified, and as far as possible the pleasant red brick which characterises Chartwell was left to speak for itself. On the opposing or east front overlooking the valley, the architect's task was less easy for the ground falls away. Here, none the less, changes of a drastic nature were made and a wing was added at right-angles containing a dining room, drawing room, and Lady Churchill's bedroom. The interior of the house now derives much of its character from these rooms. Both on this wing and on the south a high crow-stepped gable was added, probably to accentuate the pronounced vertical lines.

Perhaps Philip Tilden did not find an altogether satisfactory solution to the architectural problem which confronted him on the east and south fronts, but he produced an eminently comfortable house, one in which a man could live, and work, and bring up a family. These were his client's primary requirements. To satisfy them, the inside of Chartwell was remodelled. The 'panelled lounge hall', the dining room and the drawing room, referred to in the auction particulars of 1921, were swept away. Dining room and drawing room were now situated in the new wing, and on the first floor was created a study with open timbered roof. It was to play a significant role both in the history and literature of the next decades. From a dealer in the North End Road came panelled oak doors of about 1720, with bolection mouldings. The new house – for it was virtually that – proved so well adapted to the pur-

16

poses of the family for which it was rebuilt that it subsequently remained unaltered.

The setting of Chartwell had captured Churchill's imagination. He was determined to make the most of it. In the new house six doors gave on the garden. It is difficult to think of another house where outside and inside meet so easily, and which is so intimately linked with its surroundings. From every window one is conscious of the landscape. On the entrance front, a noble beech hangar rises steeply beyond the lawn to the skyline; eastward the land drops dramatically to combe and water; and southward stretch the distances of the Weald. Almost at once Churchill ordered a large consignment of fruit trees – quinces, damsons, plums, pears, apples and Kentish cobs – two hundred strawberry runners and three hundred asparagus plants. As will appear, there is hardly a detail of the lay-out which does not reflect the affection and activity of the owner. In its natural setting of combe and woods, it took the impress of its new master as forcibly as did the house.

Churchill, as we have seen, was rarely at Chartwell during the war and the house was closed. In 1945, after the fateful election in July, he decided to sell the property. Perhaps he was momentarily disillusioned. Also, the reopening of a country house was a formidable task for Lady Churchill in the conditions that then prevailed. Such houses were a burden, and many were coming on the market. However, a group of close friends felt that Chartwell, which for over twenty years had played so important a role in the history of the country, should be preserved for the nation. They bought Chartwell and gave it to the National Trust on the understanding that Churchill should live there undisturbed for his lifetime. The purchasers were anonymous and desired to remain so. They ensured that Churchill should enjoy the house he loved for a further twenty years and that the nation should ultimately possess a fit memorial to the foremost statesman of the twentieth century.

The house was soon reopened and came to play as important a role in Churchill's later years as it had done in the twenties and thirties. Already before the war, Churchill had acquired from his friend Sir Ian Hamilton a herd of Belted Galloway cattle whose distinctive dress was a feature of the park. Now, when opportunity arose, he bought Chartwell Farm, some 400 acres, immediately to the south, where Christopher and Mary Soames were to live, and where, until its sale in

1957, the knowledge and interest of the future Minister of Agriculture found practical expression on a mixed Kentish farm.

After Churchill's death in January 1965, the plan long envisaged came into operation and the National Trust was charged with the task of opening Chartwell to the public. Temporary changes, such as infirmity must bring about, had taken place in the arrangements at Chartwell during the last year or two of Churchill's life. The house in some degree had come to reflect his old age. With the help of Lady Churchill and Lady Soames, the balance was redressed. Chartwell once more took on the aspect of the family home which Churchill had known before the war. It was an unusual home, a place where monumental works of history were written, and where almost alone in England the political future was clearly read and the dangers that threatened the country were confronted. Chartwell was opened to the public in the summer of 1966. By the end of October in that year nearly a hundred and fifty thousand people had come to see it.

3. The Approach

In Churchill's view 'the substitution of the internal combustion engine for the horse marked a very gloomy milestone in the progress of mankind'. It is on account of the combustion engine that the visitor is constrained to enter the grounds of Chartwell some way north of the house through a car park. There could be worse avenues of approach, for the qualities of the Chartwell landscape are immediately apparent from this point. At eye level the encircling woods embrace the combe; below, its smooth pastures sweep to the lakes; more trees, and the tiled roofs of farm and cottages, preface the extended view over the Weald. The house and garden still lie hidden by the slope of the land and banks of green foliage. Both are revealed gradually. A visit to Chartwell is a progressive unfolding.

Horticulturally there are more remarkable gardens in Kent, but perhaps none so skilfully integrates the work of man and nature. The Churchills, appreciating the unique quality of the combe, wisely saw their garden, and kept it, as an extension of its natural setting. In places the sward is allowed to fall without interruption from the banking trees to the water far below. Elsewhere formal terraces provide a restful counter-point to the sweep of the valley. Even the northern walled garden (the small rose-garden) gains half its charm from a sense of enclosure upon the edge of space.

At the entrance to the garden, the house appears, somewhat to the right, half-obscured by massive banks of rhododendrons. Ahead, the gigantic leaves of a clump of *gunnera manicata* make a dark patch of green, and a bank of dwarf juniper and cotoneaster leads the eye to a cedar of Lebanon. To the left, shorn and open pasture falls to a circular swimming pool built in the thirties and to two lakes at the bottom of the combe. The swimming pool was heated, an arrangement still unusual in this country at the time, and Churchill's friends maintained that the boilers were capacious enough to heat the Ritz Hotel. These water-works are fed from the Chart Well, whose waters come purling down through rocks, fern-fringed channels and small shaded pools. Three laden rail-trucks brought the rocks from Cumberland. The elaboration of this scheme was one of Churchill's chief preoccupations and pleasures at Chartwell. When he bought the property, there was only the lower lake, and even its wooded island, originally a peninsula, was his creation. Concerned about an adequate water-supply for his schemes, he had recourse to a scientist, his friend Professor Lindemann, who assured him that the 'Well' would yield a sufficient flow. 'I am so grateful to you', Churchill wrote in May 1928, 'for the wonderful calculations you have made. . . . I hope the water will be flowing into the upper lake by the end of the week.' It still does.

To Churchill, with his love of wild life, lakes were incomplete without birds. In due course Canada geese arrived and black swans, a gift from the Australian Commonwealth. Unfortunately the black swans also attracted foxes from the surrounding woods. This created a dilemma. Neither the sportsman nor the man who was unwilling to carve a Chartwell bird at dinner, remarking, 'This goose was a friend of mine', would readily see foxes shot below the house. Thus, although the London Zoo was consulted and experiment made with protective devices, the cygnets were often taken before they were fledged. A fox-proof fence has since been set round the upper lake and the swans are now undisturbed.

From the entrance to the garden a flagged path climbs to the right. On one side rises a towering *librocedrus decurrens*; on the other past fine *magnolia soulangeana* a smaller path leads to the Goldfish Pond. Embowered by trees, among them a vast *pinus cephalonica*, and fringed by bamboo, cotoneaster, wistaria, acers and a *hydrangea paniculata*, this retired pool is deeply evocative. It was here that Churchill, particularly in later years, came regularly after lunch to sit and feed his golden orfe. His garden chair stands beside the pond and, though empty, his ample presence still seems to fill it, while his gleaming carp, those long-lived fish, still cruise the unruffled water. Such is the impress of habit that they glide expectantly towards the casual visitor as though a lesser hand might scatter the maggots, regularly despatched from Yorkshire, that they were long accustomed to receive from a prime minister. 'They are twenty years old', he once said, 'and will see me out.' They will also see out many of those who observe them curiously today. If the twentieth century can apprehend a numen, this place is hallowed ground. Here the aged statesman sat in contemplation, and here he must often have reflected on his long career and the mutability of human fortune, on the brevity of fame and the span of eternity.

Return to the garden path momentarily seems a return from timelessness to time. Between the garden wall built of Kentish ragstone and a cryptomeria (like all the giant trees it pays tribute to the Victorian owners of Chartwell), the path leads to a second pool and a bed whose white foxgloves and blue anchusa are a traditional feature of the garden in June. This water-garden was one of Lady Churchill's happiest inspirations. The path then swings up a flight of steps to the front of the house. Here, where the garden borders the road, were once sombre laurels and rhododendrons and the dark shade of conifers. The open lawn, flanked by two vast limes that hum with bees when in flower, was Churchill's creation. It was in one of these limes that he built a treehouse for his children. Even the wall, now enveloped in *clematis montana*, reflects his personality, and the story of its building has significance in view of his passion for brick-laying. Returning late one night by motor from London, he stopped in Westerham outside Quebec House, General Wolfe's birthplace. 'That', he said, looking at the wall, 'is what I want.' So the wall at Westerham with its dentils surmounted by a sloping top was reproduced at Chartwell, and now recalls not only its builder but the general who won Quebec.

After the war, Churchill often insisted that the oak gates on the road should remain open. This was a cause of concern to the men charged with security at Chartwell, but the insistence was characteristic. It reflected a wish to remain accessible to his neighbours and the people of Westerham. Sometimes the curious who came to look would be welcomed and taken to see the goldfish.

The west front of the house as seen from the lawn derives much of its architectural character from its pleasant brick-work and from the brick-moulded mullions and transoms of the windows. The five central bays are of older brick and indicate the dimensions of the pre-nineteenth-century house which was subsequently enlarged. A comparison of Plates on page 15 reveals the extensive changes made by Churchill in the early twenties. The Victorian design was radically simplified and a straight roof-line was introduced over the six central bays. Only one of the gables was retained (that at the southern end) and with the disappearance of a central gable went a large entrance porch and an oriel above. Another oriel disappeared on the projecting front under the southern gable. At the north end of the house the window bays of vaguely Tudor character were carried up a third storey, which enabled the architect to dispense with a dormer window. The chimney stacks were also rebuilt and panelled in classical fashion. The surround to the front door came from a London dealer. Age has beautifully silvered the wood. With elaborately foliated pilasters and involuted scrolls at its base, the composition strikes a baroque note and must surely have once framed a doorway in the interior of some great mansion in the first half of the eighteenth century.

4. Inside the House

CHURCHILL was not a collector and he had little interest in works of art. Thus few of the contents of Chartwell, apart from a number of pieces bought by Lady Churchill, are intrinsically important. They derive their interest from the man to whom they belonged and because they represent *his* choice. He surrounded himself with objects that he liked and because he was a man of sentiment he tended to like things for their association. When late in life he received presents from admirers all over the world, it was usually the giver rather than the gift that mattered. Because Churchill was uninfluenced by contemporary taste, Chartwell has proved impervious to passing fashion. Never following the mode of the moment, it could not become outmoded. A house designed to live and work in, it possesses a timeless quality.

THE HALL

A painting by Churchill (No. 377) provides an appropriate introduction.* Dating from about 1948, and signed with the initials 'WSC', it depicts the statue of a seated Buddha and red amaryllis lilies on a table. The subject illustrates the quality of personal association which often meant so much to Churchill. The statue was a bequest from General Sir Ian Hamilton (1853–1947), a friend since the distant nineties and the general who in the First World War commanded the expeditionary force which attempted the capture of Gallipoli. The first amaryllis lilies arrived at Chartwell as the gift of Princess Marina, Duchess of Kent, soon after the war when Churchill was ill. They prospered in the glasshouses and became one of his favourite flowers.

Beyond the glass doors which give on the Inner Hall hangs a mono-

*For details of the Churchill paintings see Appendix I, p. 58.

chrome oil-sketch of the front door by William Nicholson (1872–1949). It is undated but was probably painted in the course of a long stay at Chartwell in 1933. Lady Churchill admired Nicholson's work and bought several of his paintings. The English wall-mirror in walnut frame is a reproduction of an early-eighteenth-century design. In a mahogany umbrella stand are some of Churchill's many walking-sticks. They include a gold-topped malacca cane presented to him by the United States Air Force, a stick with a silver band made from bog oak many hundred years old discovered in the course of the excavation of the South Albert Dock in 1915, and an aluminium shooting-stick with a comfortable seat which Churchill used in his last years when walking round the garden.

On the wall to the left hangs a view of the port of Antwerp by J. Opsomer, the gift of the City of Antwerp. On the panelled oak chest below stands a bronze which represents the ideal thoroughbred horse. It is by Herbert Hazeltine (1877–1962), an American sculptor who worked in Paris and whose treatment of such subjects was outstanding in his generation. It is inscribed 'The Thoroughbred Horse. To Winston Churchill.' and is signed and dated 1949. On the same chest lies the Visitors' Book. In spite of the signatures of the great and famous, this record of comings and goings at Chartwell strongly reflects the family life of a country house. The blotched and tentative signatures of children, of nephews and nieces, and later of grandchildren, recur. The first name – June 1924 – is that of Mrs Bertram Romilly, Lady Churchill's sister, whose two brilliant and wayward sons Esmond and Giles were to make an impact on the imagination of many young men at the time of the Spanish Civil War. In the first year, visitors to Chartwell included Lloyd George, Balfour, Admiral Sir Roger Keyes, Sir Archibald Sinclair, Lord Carson, Lord Birkenhead, and two other friends who, many years later, were to play important roles in the Second World War – Brendan Bracken and Frederick Lindemann. The precise, cramped signature of 'the Prof', as Lindemann was affectionately known by his friends, was to occur more often than any other in the Visitors' Book. He was at Chartwell over the weekend of August 28th 1939, and his is the last signature before war put an end to the entries and to life at Chartwell for several years.

The Visitors' Book resumes in January 1946 and the second name is that of Lord Ismay, who had been Deputy Secretary to the War Cabinet throughout Churchill's administration. The record closes in October 1964 when Churchill, already failing, left Chartwell for the last time. There is something touching in the fact that the most frequent signature in the final months was that of Field-Marshal Montgomery, the general to whom he owed his most striking military victories.

In the small lobby that gives access to the Drawing Room hang a painting of Mrs Bertram Romilly in fancy dress by Neville Lytton (*c.* 1910), and a charcoal drawing of Churchill in his robes as Chancellor of the Exchequer by John Sargent, R.A. (1856–1925).

THE DRAWING ROOM

This is one of the three rooms, looking over the garden and the Weald, contrived by Tilden in the projecting east wing to which Churchill sometimes referred as 'my promontory'. The room conveys an impression of clarity and light. The prismatic drops and festoons of the eighteenth-century chandeliers glow like transparent fruit, and when the windows are open the flowers on the chintz curtains stir. Guests, as they gathered here before dinner on summer evenings, must have found it a delightful room.

The large boldly patterned carpet is a nineteenth-century Mahal. Two mirrors of George II design on either side of the east window reflect the room and seem to extend it. They hang above a pair of mid-eighteenth-century walnut side-tables whose tops are inlaid with medallions in satinwood. The powder blue vases mounted as lamps are K'ang Hsi (1662–1722). Between the side-tables, and a little in front, is a Georgian mahogany card table. It is set for Bezique, a game which Churchill enjoyed and which in later years he often played, and intently played, at this table with Lady Churchill and his guests. It was characteristic that whatever he did, whatever he undertook, whether it was a hand of cards or the direction of an empire, received his close attention.

Paintings by Churchill hang on the right-hand wall (Nos. 6, 361), but the place of honour is occupied by a Claude Monet (1840–1926), an oil painting of London Bridge done in 1907. In the early years of the century Monet was often in London painting winter views of the Thames, many of them from his balcony in the Savoy Hotel. This painting was given by Mr Emery Reves, who after the war bought the foreign translation rights in Churchill's books. Below is a mahogany *bureau à cylindre* in the Louis XVI style. Upon it stands an agreeable mid-nineteenth-century Staffordshire pottery representation of St George and the Dragon. This conjunction well illustrates Chartwell's disregard for fashion and the preoccupations of the connoisseur. The French bureau is flanked by a gift from the City of Worcester: a mahogany Pembroke table banded in satinwood, the top inlaid with the city arms. Beyond, in front of the bookcase, is a Regency black lacquer table with Chinoiserie decoration which, it has been reasonably suggested, may have come from the Brighton Pavilion. The head of Edward VIII on the window-sill, cast in tangum alloy, was a present on Churchill's eightieth birthday. At the time of the Abdication he was among the few politicians to appreciate the difficulty of the King's position and to speak on his behalf. After Churchill's death the King, as Duke of Windsor, was to write: 'One of the pleasures of being a Britisher in the Twentieth Century has been the privilege of sharing that century with Sir Winston Churchill.'

Grouped round the fireplace are sofas and chairs, comfortable provision for family and friends. Beyond the further sofa on a mahogany card-table, and seeming to survey the room with a certain Gallic detachment, is a fine crystal cock by Lalique, the gift of President de Gaulle to Lady Churchill. Beside the sofa is a mahogany tripod table with 'pie-crust' border. It is the sort of table on which, since the mid-eighteenth century, host and guest have found it convenient to place a glass of brandy or balance a cigar. Churchill often did so, for his preferred seat was the yellow armchair beside it.

On the left-hand wall of the Drawing Room, on either side of the fireplace, are paintings by Churchill (Nos. 298, 319, 317). On the modern chimney-piece of late eighteenth-century design are two Paris vases, probably made shortly after the Revolution. They are filled with flowers. The latter were always an essential feature of the rooms at Chartwell. Above the mantelshelf, looking across at Monet's vision of London Bridge, hangs an oil of Colonist II, Churchill's wonder colt. It was painted in 1951 by Raoul Millais, a grandson of the Pre-Raphaelite master. 'No hour of life is lost', Churchill said, 'that is spent in the saddle.' He was among the finest polo players of his generation and as a cabinet minister in the Liberal Government of 1906 found time to play first-class polo. He described it as the 'emperor of games' and played for the last time in Malta in 1927. He was also a rider to hounds and on his seventy-fourth birthday turned out at Chartwell with the Old Surrey and Burstow.

Though it was not until after the Second World War that Churchill became a serious racehorse owner, racing was in the blood. Lord Randolph's Abbesse de Jouarre – familiarly known in the stables as 'Abscess of the Jaw' – had won the Oaks, and when staying at Warwick Castle in 1902 Churchill surprised the Aga Khan and his fellow-guests by reciting the names of the last fifty Derby winners and their breeding. It was one of those unusual feats of memory of which he remained capable even in old age. Nearly fifty years later, influenced by his son-in-law Christopher Soames, he set up a racing stable and in 1949 registered his father's colours, pink and chocolate. His horses were sent to Walter Nightingall, who trained them with notable success. Colonist II, a French-bred colt, was bought as a maiden three-year-old and won £13,000 in prize money. Later Churchill bought a stud-farm not far away at Lingfield. Among well-known horses bred there and raced in his colours were Welsh Abbot, Tudor Monarch, High Hat and Vienna. In all he won seventy-two races and £100,000 in stakes over a period of sixteen years, a remarkable record for a small stud.

Nearer the door is a half-length oil of Lady Churchill, painted in 1946 by Douglas Chandor. The blue-glazed earthenware vase mounted as a lamp on the table below was bought by Lady Churchill in Morocco in 1943. On the shelves near by are copies of some of Churchill's works, and on the adjoining table the little marble bust of Napoleon bears an uncanny resemblance to Churchill. Two of his paintings hang on the west wall (Nos. 259, 383).

In the inner hall between the Drawing Room and the Library hang a seascape by Churchill (No. 103), a portrait of Diana and Sarah Churchill as girls by Charles Sims, R.A. (1873–1928) – presented to the National Trust in 1966 by Mr H. R. H. Everest – and two views of the old Chamber of the House of Commons, one a coloured engraving of 1741–2 probably by John Pyne, and the other an aquatint of 1835 by Samuel Cousins after a painting by D. W. Burgess. The Chamber was destroyed by fire in 1834 and rebuilt after 1840 to designs by Augustus Pugin and Charles Barry. The interior was again gutted by enemy bombs in May 1941. (The painted shield which hangs with the Pyne engraving is believed to be the sole surviving relic from the interior of the Chamber.) The foundation stone of the present Chamber, designed by

THE DRAWING ROOM

Courtesy of Keystone Press Agency

CHURCHILL'S STUDY

Courtesy of G. P. King

Sir Giles Gilbert Scott, was laid on 26th May 1948. At the ceremony Churchill, then Leader of the Opposition, referred to the House as a living and deathless entity, the guardian of free debate and of our constitutional liberties.

THE LIBRARY

'Nothing', said Churchill, 'makes a man more reverent than a library.' He combined an abiding respect for books as the repositories of the thought and wisdom of great men, with an enthusiastic appreciation of the possibilities of his native tongue. Like Wellington, he plunged into history as a subaltern in India – 'my life would be intolerable here', he wrote in 1897, 'were it not for the consolation of literature' – and he later became widely read in the subjects which interested him, making a specialised collection of books relating to Napoleon. He found a fascination in books as material objects and expressed a sentiment familiar to many book lovers:

> If you cannot read all your books, at any rate handle, or as it were, fondle them – peer into them, let them fall open where they will, read from the first sentence that arrests the eye, set them back on the shelves with your own hands, arrange them on your own plan so that if you do not know what is in them, you at least know where they are. Let them be your friends; let them at any rate be your acquaintances.

Churchill's reading was reinforced by unusual powers of assimilation and by an extraordinary memory. He could recite long passages of verse which he had not read for decades. Apart from history, which was his concern both as author and statesman, he was perhaps most at home with the writers of the Augustan age with whom he had an instinctive sympathy. Gibbon, who influenced his own writing, was a particular favourite. Curiously enough, it was only late in life that he developed a taste for Victorian novelists like the Brontës and Trollope. Of the Trollope novels he preferred *The Duke's Children*.

Though this was not the room where Churchill wrote, it was here that he came to consult when the need arose – no doubt using the Library steps that stand in one corner – the books that were not at hand in his Study.

Though books are the heart of the matter, there is much else here that is evocative. Set into one of the bookshelves is a relief model of

Port Arromanches in Normandy, as it appeared on D plus 109 days (September 23rd 1944). The artificial harbours to which Churchill had given so much thought proved a complete success. The assault force of the operation 'Overlord' consisting of 176,000 men and 2,000 vehicles began to disembark according to plan on June 6th. Within a week Churchill himself was in France.

Facing the relief of Port Arromanches hangs a half-length portrait of Churchill in 1942, seated at his desk in his blue siren suit. Executed with more realism than sensitivity, it is the work of Frank Salisbury (1874–1962), a successful official portraitist. The bookshelves to its left are filled with editions of Churchill's works in translation. His writings were published in Japanese, Arabic and a dozen other languages. On the shelf below these translations is a bust of Roosevelt (the gift of Averill Harriman) and a scale model of 'Roaring Meg', the cannon which played an important role in the siege of Londonderry in 1688–9. It was presented to Churchill with the freedom of the city.

Bookshelves allow space for only one other painting, a panel depicting St John the Baptist. This ikon was given to Churchill by Archbishop Damaskinos, head of the Greek Orthodox Church, when he visited a distressed and faction-torn Greece in the winter of 1944. The Archbishop, a sturdy patriot and shrewd politician, had co-operated with the right-wing resistance movement, and on the collapse and withdrawal of the German forces was for a time regent and the most powerful figure in the country.

Between the windows is a mirror in an Italian seventeenth-century giltwood frame, and below, on the writing table, are signed photographs of King George VI and Queen Elizabeth. Churchill was a monarchist. His remark that 'No institution pays such dividends' was the rationalisation of an almost religious belief. Indeed, the royal family was a subject on which he would hear no criticism. It was on the night of May 10th 1940, when the Germans were advancing across Europe, that he was summoned to the palace and asked to form a government. Throughout the difficult years that followed he had the King's close confidence.

After the war he wrote, 'I regarded as a signal honour the gracious intimacy with which I, as First Minister, was treated, for which I suppose there has been no precedent since the days of Queen Anne and Marlborough during his years of power.' He was deeply moved by the

King's death in 1952 and the Government wreath at his funeral bore in Churchill's hand the words 'For Valour', the inscription on the Victoria Cross.

The Persian carpet in this room is of Tabriz manufacture and the two Georgian mahogany armchairs upholstered in leather date from the middle of the eighteenth century. The elephant-size despatch box behind the door stood on the table of the House of Commons from June 1941 to October 1950 and was presented to Churchill as a memento of those historic years.

The staircase outside the Library was built in 1966 to replace back-stairs too cramped to take the flow of traffic anticipated when the house opened to visitors. Here are a painting of a turkey, probably by Hondecoeter (1636–1695), and cartoons by David Low, E. H. Shepherd, and Edward Ardizzone. Churchill wrote that he 'always loved cartoons', and he never seems to have resented cartoonists however critical they might be. Low, whose political sympathies lay far to the Left, he regarded as the greatest cartoonist of his day, a Charlie Chaplin of caricature, whose ready pencil was able to deal equally well with tragedy or comedy.

On the stairs are photographs of a number of Churchill's close friends. They mainly date from the years before the Second World War.

On the left of the passage leading to Lady Churchill's bedroom is Oscar Nemon's maquette of the statue of Churchill in the House of Commons.

LADY CHURCHILL'S BEDROOM

This room, with its barrel-vaulted ceiling, became the dining room in Churchill's last years, but has now been carefully restored as it was before the war. Against the left-hand wall stands a late-seventeenth-century walnut armoire, probably Italian, its front treated classically with cornice, fluted pilasters, and Ionic capitals. On either side, behind *blanc de Chine* figures of the maternal goddess Kwan Yin, hang portraits of Blanche Stanley, Countess of Airlie, Lady Churchill's grandmother, and of her daughter Sarah (the original by John Merton). Two gouaches by Sarah Churchill painted in 1957 show her beach chalet – by day and by moonlight – at Malibou in California. Two alcoves, one in this wall and one opposite, contain a collection of equestrian figures in porcelain.

31

One represents Napoleon, and the others illustrate the uniforms of officers and non-commissioned officers of the Imperial Army. They were a bequest to Lady Churchill from Lord Bracken. The figures are of German make from the factory set up by Carl Thieme at Potschappel near Dresden in 1875.

The eighteenth-century stone fireplace was introduced by Philip Tilden when the room was built. The drum-shaped Louis XVI clock surmounted by an eagle is by Gavelle l'Ainé, a maker active about 1780, and belonged to Lady Randolph Churchill. Above it hangs a mid-eighteenth-century gilt gesso mirror.

On the shelves on either side of the fireplace are family photographs and drawings. To the left: below a drawing of Lady Churchill's grandmother (the Countess of Airlie) are her husband, her daughter Mary (Lady Soames) with her two eldest children, and her granddaughter Celia Sandys (now Mrs Walters). In front on the circular mahogany table is a photograph of Randolph Churchill with June, his second wife, and their daughter Arabella. To the right: below a chalk drawing of Lady Churchill's eldest daughter Diana Sandys by Geoffroy Dechaume are her daughter Sarah (Lady Audley), and a photograph of a painting by Oswald Birley of Mary Soames, her youngest daughter.

On the dressing-table is a Victorian silver-mounted crystal dressing set engraved with cypher and coronet which belonged to the Countess of Airlie, Lady Churchill's grandmother. The two cut-glass decanters with silver stoppers engraved with a coronet and the letter 'M', for Marlborough, were a postwar gift to Churchill.

The centre of the room is occupied by a mahogany knee-hole writing desk, at which stands a Regency chair with 'sabre' legs of about 1820. On the desk stands Lady Churchill's favourite photograph of her husband, and a charming pencil drawing by John Tenniel of Churchill as a boy, done in 1890.

The four-poster bed, hung with moiré silk, is flanked by two urn-shaped French Empire bed tables in walnut.

THE ANTEROOM

This small room, originally a bathroom, has been arranged to display china, medals, and other Churchilliana.

On the left-hand wall are photographs of many of the generals and admirals – British, American, and French – associated with Churchill in the Second World War. As no previous prime minister had done, Churchill participated with his general staff in devising strategy and elaborating tactics. He was in constant touch, submitting detailed and technical memoranda in every field of operation. General Eisenhower noted that he 'maintained such close contact with all operations as to make him a virtual member of the British Chiefs of Staff'. Many of the men whose signed photographs hang here were thus not only the instruments of his high policy but over a long period his associates in counsel.

The Georgian mahogany cabinet contains a display of china. On the top shelf is late Royal Crown Derby and on the second a Russian tea service, dated 1945, decorated with views of Leningrad, and presented to Lady Churchill by the Mayor of Leningrad. On the third shelf is a Dresden coffee set, richly gilded on apple green ground, and painted with portraits of Napoleon, and ladies of the Imperial court. Many of the pieces bear the mark (the letters 'RK' with a crown) of R. Klemm, a decorator working at Dresden after 1868.

The portrait medallions from left to right represent: Queen Hortense, Napoleon's step-daughter who married his brother Louis Napoleon, King of Holland (1806–10), and was the mother of Napoleon III; Leontine Metternich, daughter of Prince Metternich; Eliza Bonaparte, the Emperor's sister, born in Ajaccio in 1772; Napoleon; the Empress Josephine, widow of the Vicomte de Beauharnais (executed in 1794) and Napoleon's first wife, whom he divorced for dynastic reasons in 1809 and whose memory at the Château de Malmaison still evokes a vanished charm and beauty; Pauline Bonaparte, Napoleon's favourite and youngest sister, who married Prince Borghese and was immortalised in the sculptures of Canova; and Countess Schlick.

The rest of the cabinet contains part of three very similar Sèvres dinner services, with gilt decoration and the cypher of Napoleon III on a white ground. Most of the pieces date from the mid-nineteenth century. A fascinating story attaches to their acquisition. Clara Jerome, Churchill's grandmother, was in Paris in May 1871 when the mob fired and pillaged the Tuileries. Many of the contents were auctioned outside the burning palace, and there in the cinder-laden air Mrs Jerome bought part of the Imperial service, bringing it back to her apartment in the Boulevard Haussman on a hired wheelbarrow.

33

Beside the china cabinet hangs the famous letter addressed to 'A certain Naval Person' which Roosevelt sent by the hand of Wendel Wilkie in June 1941. It brought an assurance of sympathy from across the Atlantic at a time when it was much needed. Six months later the United States came into the war.

Copies of two other documents no less historic hang on the right-hand wall: the Prime Minister's terse directive to Field-Marshal Alexander, drafted in Cairo in August 1942, instructing him to expel the German and Italian forces from North Africa, and the Field-Marshal's telegram, no less terse, informing the Prime Minister in 1943 that the order had been successfully carried out. On the same wall hang signed photographs of the Allied generals with whom Churchill was associated in the First World War.

The mahogany spinet banded with satinwood, and converted as a display cabinet, houses a collection of commemorative medals, mainly associated with the Second World War.

On the landing outside are seven paintings by Churchill (Nos. 4, 7, 68, 96, 154, 415, 459) and the two chairs used by Winston Churchill and Lady Churchill in Westminster Abbey at the coronation of King George VI in 1937.

THE MUSEUM ROOM

This room and the adjoining Uniform Room were made out of three guest bedrooms in 1966.

The life-size photographs which cover two walls portray Churchill from childhood to old age. In the first he is standing with his mother, the beautiful Lady Randolph Churchill, who had been Jennie Jerome of New York; in the last he is sitting quietly in the garden at Chartwell with the work of a lifetime behind him. The isolated photograph by the far doorway shows him from behind in dressing gown and ten-gallon hat painting in the south of France.

The powerful bronze portrait-bust standing against the end wall is by his cousin Clare Sheridan, daughter of Clara Jerome (Mrs Moreton Frewen), and was done in 1942. It clearly shows the small scar on his forehead which he carried after a serious taxi-accident in New York in 1931. When sitting for this bust he thought the sculptress was over-emphasising the famous bull-dog look, and said with a smile, 'Forget

Mussolini, and remember that I am a servant of the House of Commons.'

The showcases are devoted mainly to the display of gifts made to Churchill in the last twenty years of his life and have been lent by Lady Churchill. The donors range from peoples, potentates and prime ministers to corporations and societies. They include the United States of America and associations as modest as the Hastings Winkle Club of which Churchill was a member. Among the most attractive exhibits are the two gold cups given by King George VI and Queen Elizabeth, the simple silver-gilt casket presented with the freedom of the City of Westminster, the crystal cross of Lorraine from President de Gaulle, the green-glazed Persian pottery bowl from President Roosevelt, and the silver box designed as a shako which Churchill received on his eightieth birthday from the officers of his old regiment. Some of the other gifts, it must be confessed, are a greater tribute to the donors' affection and regard than to their taste. It is a solemn thought that Marshal Stalin, with the resources of an empire behind him, should have given his most eminent contemporary the silver and crystal bowls displayed, or that the wealth of the Belgian Congo, in a day when it was still rich, should have found expression in the ivory and malachite cigar box on view. The thought is one that it would be invidious to pursue further, but it implies something significant about the official taste of the twentieth century.

There is another type of tribute here more important and moving than gold or silver. In the wall cases are three documents which illustrate the unique position held by Churchill in the esteem and affection of his fellow citizens and the western world: his honorary American citizenship, his Nobel prize for literature, and the volume which records the tribute of the House of Commons on his eightieth birthday.

THE UNIFORM ROOM

On the right-hand wall a life-size photograph shows Churchill taking leave of the Queen after she had dined with him at Downing Street on April 4th 1955 on the eve of his resignation as prime minister. In the showcase below are the insignia of the Order of the Garter: with the inscription *Honi soit qui mal y pense*. They are those with which Churchill was invested as knight companion by the Queen in April 1953. His installation in the Garter Chapel at Windsor took place in the following year. In accordance with custom the insignia and the robes were returned on Churchill's death. The insignia have been graciously lent by Her Majesty the Queen.

The Order of the Garter, the most coveted of the English Orders of Chivalry, and one of the oldest orders in Europe, dates from the reign of Edward III. Its members consist of the sovereign and twenty-nine knight companions, together with such members of the royal family as may be appointed.

The insignia of some of the other orders of which Churchill was a member are shown on the shelves below the display cases. The cases themselves contain some of Churchill's robes and uniforms. Starting from the left these are:

1. Undress uniform of a Captain of Trinity House

This ancient fraternity obtained its first charter from Henry VIII in 1514. It was primarily to act 'for the relief, increase, and augmentation of the Shipping of this Realm of England'. Today the duties of the corporation of Trinity House are the administration of lighthouses, lightships, and seamarks, and the control of pilotage. It is responsible for some 90 lighthouses and 40 lightships. There are at present rather over twenty Elder Brethren of Trinity House.

Churchill became an Elder Brother in 1913 when First Lord of the Admiralty. The office appealed to his sense of the romantic, and he often wore the impressive full dress uniform (p. 38) on state occasions. (It is worth recording that on naval occasions he habitually wore a short double-breasted blue coat with the cap of the Royal Yacht Squadron.)

2. Service Dress of an Air Commodore of the Royal Auxiliary Air Force

The Royal Auxiliary Air Force was founded in 1924. Churchill was appointed Honorary Air Commodore of 615 (County of Surrey) Squadron in April 1939. He had close and early links with flying. His prescience, which also led to the creation of the tank, foresaw the importance of air power long before the First World War. In his own words, he was from 1911 to 1915 'responsible for the creation and development of the Royal Naval Air Service; from July 1917 to the end of the war he was in charge of the design, manufacture, and supply of all kinds of aircraft . . . ; and from 1919 to 1921 he was Air Minister'.

He flew his first plane in 1912. 'The air', as he said, 'is an extremely dangerous, jealous, and exacting mistress', and the pronouncement is borne out by the fact that he had two crashes in his early flying days. He also coined the word 'seaplane'.

3. Robes of the Chancellor of Bristol University

Churchill became Chancellor of Bristol University in 1929 and held the office until his death. He was also Rector of Aberdeen and Edinburgh Universities, and received twenty-one honorary degrees from universities all over the world.

4. Full dress of a Privy Councillor, and cocked hat with ostrich plume

The Privy Council has a long history. In the Middle Ages it consisted simply of the sovereign's chief advisers and was often the effective instrument of government. Since the reign of George I the Council has been merely a formal body transacting formal business, though the sovereign refers certain matters to standing committees of the Council (such as the Judicial Committee) or to committees set up for a special purpose. All members of the cabinet are privy councillors, and in recent years there have usually been about three hundred councillors. The office has long been honorific.

Churchill's appointment dates from 1907 when he was thirty-three and was in office for the first time as Under-Secretary for the Colonies.

5. Tropical Service dress with regimental badges

This uniform was probably first worn by Churchill in Cairo in 1942. The badges are those of the Royal Sussex Regiment.

6. Full dress of the Lord Warden of the Cinque Ports and a silver-gilt nef presented to Churchill with the freedom of Hastings in 1947

The Romans created a special system of defence for the south-east coast, which was particularly vulnerable to attack from the Baltic. This was afterwards adapted by the Saxons and was based on the five ports – 'cinque ports' – of Hastings, New Romney, Hythe, Dover and Sandwich. William the Conqueror maintained and reconstituted the system and the towns of Winchelsea and Rye were later added. Until 1855 the ancient office of Warden of the Cinque Ports carried considerable powers.

Churchill was appointed Lord Warden of the Cinque Ports and Constable of Dover Castle in 1941 and was installed by the Grand Court of Shepway in August 1946. He was the first commoner to hold the office.

7. Full dress uniform of an Elder Brother of Trinity House, and a silver demi-lion rampant on a drum plinth

The Lion (the Trinity House crest) was presented to Churchill by the Elder Brethren on his eightieth birthday.

8. Siren suit, ten-gallon hat and slippers embroidered in gold thread with the initials 'WSC'

Long before the war Churchill wore denim boiler-suits for brick-laying and working at Chartwell. During the war he adopted them as practical and comfortable, and christened them 'Siren Suits'. He later had them made in velvet, chiefly to wear in the evening at home.

The 'ten-gallon' hat was often worn by Churchill when painting in the open in the south of France or at home. At Chartwell the hat was always adorned with a swan or goose feather.

9. Facsimile Garter robes and bonnet and eighteenth-century star of the Order

The robes and bonnet are lent by Madame Tussaud's.

The star is that which belonged to the 1st Duke of Marlborough.

10. Service dress of a full Colonel in the 4th Queen's Own Hussars, and (below) a number of Churchill's medals*

The creation of the 4th Hussars was the direct outcome of the Monmouth Rebellion. Parliament, thoroughly alarmed, authorised James II to raise twenty regiments, and on July 17th 1685, twelve days after the battle of Sedgemoor, a commission was given to Colonel John Berkeley to raise the regiment of dragoons that became the 4th Hussars. Originally known as Princess Anne of Denmark's Dragoons, in honour of the future Queen Anne, the regiment was raised in Somerset and Wiltshire. In its long and distinguished history it won battle honours in the Peninsula, the Crimea, Afghanistan, Flanders, Alamein and

*The medals that were presented to Churchill are in the keeping of Mr Winston Churchill. Those on display were bought by the National Trust in 1966.

Italy. In the fifties, on the reorganisation of the Army, it was amalgamated with the 8th King's Royal Irish Hussars. Churchill became Colonel of the Regiment in 1941.

Churchill received the Queen's commission in 1894 and soon after leaving Sandhurst was gazetted to the Queen's Own Hussars. He was to see battlefields in many guises and in many countries, in Cuba in 1895, with the Malakand Field Service on the North-West Frontier in 1897, at Omdurman in 1898, where he took part in the historic charge of the 21st Lancers, in the Boer War, and in Flanders in 1916. As a Minister in both wars his wish to get as close as possible to the enemy was a cause of recurrent concern to the General Staff. He was only dissuaded from sailing with the invasion fleet on 'D Day' by the direct intervention of George VI. A born soldier and strategist, he would undoubtedly have achieved the highest eminence if he had persevered in the career of his first choice, the Army.

Of the medals displayed the Queen's Sudan Medal, here associated with Churchill's role at Omdurman, and the French decorations are of particular interest. Wearing the uniform of the 4th Queen's Own Hussars, he received the Médaille Militaire from the French Prime Minister, Paul Ramadier, in Paris in 1947, and the Croix de la Libération, perhaps somewhat tardily, from the hands of de Gaulle in 1958.

Churchill was sometimes vague about orders and medals. On one occasion he arrived at the Danish Embassy wearing the sash of the Order of the Elephant, a decoration he much prized and one of the oldest in Europe, across the wrong hip. On another occasion, at a reception in Nancy, he wore the medal and ribbon of the Médaille Militaire in the right lapel. Before the evening was out every man in the room wearing the Médaille Militaire had transferred it to his right lapel. 'The French', Churchill commented, 'are the best diplomats in the world'.

11. A selection of hats

Churchill hats – his 'square' bowlers, his wide-brimmed Stetsons, and the top-hats which in early days he wore with such engaging panache – were for decades a part of his public image. The fame of Churchill's headgear dates from 1910, when as Home Secretary he went to support the Liberal Candidate at Southport in the general election. By mistake

he picked up a very small hat, not his own, and wore it without
noticing the difference when he went for a walk on the sands. Cartoonists and the press seized their opportunity.

THE STUDY

This room is the heart of Chartwell. Except during the war, Churchill
used it constantly for forty years. It bears his authentic imprint
and is essentially as he left it for the last time in October 1964. In
this room he considered his political future when, after three defeats,
he was at last re-elected to parliament in 1924; here over five years he
contemplated his policies as Chancellor of the Exchequer in Baldwin's
Government; here in the succeeding ten years, unconsidered and out
of office, he desperately reflected on the growing power of Hitler to
whose implications his countrymen seemed blind. To this room he
again returned, famous but rejected, after the electoral defeat of July
1945, and here after relinquishing the office of Prime Minister in 1954
he passed much of his old age reading and writing.

The Study was part of the Statesman's life. It was also the Author's
workshop. Like others who have played a decisive role in English
history, from Halifax and Burke to Disraeli and Derby, Churchill was
a man-of-letters. He loved both the spoken and the written word, and
he knew their power. Perhaps the most eloquent orator since Fox, he
once told the Authors' Club that 'the man who could not say what he
had to say in good English could not have very much to say that was
worth listening to'. It was at Chartwell that he took up his pen. In
addition to endless memoranda and the letters of a busy man, he wrote
or dictated in this room the last volumes of *The World Crisis, Marlborough* (of which Edward Marsh was given a first glimpse in manuscript when recuperating at Chartwell in 1932), *The Second World War,
A History of the English Speaking Peoples,* and the *Thoughts and Adventures*
which reveal so many facets of his character. All these are prefaced
from Chartwell and were largely written in this Study. Writing, to
Churchill, was not only a stimulus and almost an intoxication, so
strong was his response to the rhythm and colour of English, but a
recurrent solace in times of adversity. 'Writing a long and substantial
book', he said, 'is like having a friend and companion at your side, to
whom you can always turn for comfort and amusement.' In the years

before the war, he often needed the presence of such a friend and companion.

The Study was Philip Tilden's creation. He removed the ceiling to reveal the beams and rafters of the older building that preceded the Victorian house, and inserted the Tudor doorway with its moulded architrave. The windows look west across the lawn to the beech hangar that rises to Crockham Hill and east across the garden to the lakes. At the south end of the room, a panelled door leads to Churchill's bedroom. It is a small, simple room, almost austere, but its ample bow-window offers an unimpeded view over the Weald. So important was this view to Churchill that he permitted nothing to obscure it. Consequently, his dressing-glass was slotted to drop, when not in use, below his dressing-table, which stood in front of the window. Among the few pictures in the room are photographs of his father and mother. Asquith in 1921 when recording Lady Randolph's death in his Journal paid tribute not only to her gaiety, zest and courage, but to the fact that Churchill had always been 'the best and most devoted of sons'.

The threshold of the Study in which Churchill spent so many productive hours is an appropriate place to outline the pattern of his day at Chartwell. It has been faithfully recorded, as it was in post-war years, by the man who served as his valet from 1949 to 1952.

Churchill was called at 8 o'clock or 8.30 with a substantial English breakfast. He then read the papers – giving priority to *The Times* and *Daily Telegraph* – before settling down, still in bed with the room at a carefully controlled temperature of 74° Fahrenheit, to his morning's work. Until luncheon he wrote memoranda or dictated to one or other of his secretaries. Often he continued to dictate even while dressing. Incidentally he was perhaps the last statesman to dress with an eighteenth-century sense of style. Even his siren suits became him.

After luncheon he would walk round the garden, feed the golden orfe, and perhaps look at the waterfowl on the lakes. He would then retire to sleep for an hour or two, a habit he had first acquired in 1895 in Cuba, a country where climate imposed a siesta and custom approved it. He woke with renewed energy, and undoubtedly this break, particularly during the war, enabled him to maintain an enormous output. Often the secretaries were again summoned to his bedroom or study, where he would work until dinner.

About midnight he would retire to his Study and often more dictation followed. It would be between two and four when he went to bed. His day had rarely been less than eighteen or twenty hours, and it was not unusual for him to have dictated three or four thousand words.

The most significant feature of the Study is the wide mahogany table with claw and ball feet at which Churchill wrote. Like the mahogany bureau-bookcase with gothic glazing and elaborately crested cornice against the opposite wall, it belonged to his father, Lord Randolph Churchill, and is a good nineteenth-century reproduction of an eighteenth-century design. This table, on which both the political history of our time and the achievements of a great ancestor were recorded with authority and style, movingly reflects Churchill's affections, friendships and interests. It is dominated by photographs of his wife, his children, his grandson Winston, and his mother and her sister, Clara, when young. There is also a pencil drawing of his younger brother, John Churchill (1880–1947), to whom he was devoted; miniatures of his mother and father; and a small water-colour of a four-in-hand in Jerome Park, New York, with his maternal grandfather, Leonard Jerome, on the box. The latter, a stockbroker and financier, was founder of the American Jockey Club. A photograph of a drawing by Jocelin Bodley is tribute to his close friendship with Field-Marshal Smuts, and two porcelain busts reflect a life-long admiration for Napoleon and Nelson. The Emperor's bust in biscuit Sèvres bears the signature of Antoine-Denis Chaudet (1763–1810), and the initials 'A.B.' for Alexandre Brachard jeune who worked as a repairer at Sèvres between 1784 and 1827. The modern silver inkstand is engraved with the Churchill and Spencer crests.

On the window-sill beyond the desk are a bronze cast of Lady Randolph Churchill's hand and a fragment of a thirty-pound shrapnel which in Flanders in the First World War providentially fell between Churchill and his cousin, the 9th Duke of Marlborough. It is inscribed to Churchill with the words 'this fragment of a shell fell between us and might have separated us for ever, but is now a token of union'.

Sunny, the 9th Duke, was Churchill's life-long friend and made a substantial contribution to the expenses of his first successful election campaign at Oldham in 1900.

The bookcase at the entrance to the Study contains, as might be expected, mainly historical works. On a central shelf stands, appropriately enough, one of the most sensitive clocks devised by Swiss horologists to record the passage of time whose great moments are history. The movement by Jaeger-le-Coultre is perpetual and is motivated by changes in atmospheric pressure.

Beyond the bookcase in the corner hangs a shield with the armoury of Malta, given by the people of the island, and below it a representation on vellum of Churchill's orders, decorations and medals.

On the right, beyond Lord Randolph's bureau-bookcase which contains the 'secret' drawers often incorporated in such pieces, is a Chippendale mahogany card table on which are despatch boxes and papers relating to the official history of the Second World War. The mahogany lectern against the wall – a standing desk such as Disraeli used at Hughenden Manor – replaces a simple unvarnished desk of similar design made to Churchill's specifications. It was a present from his children in 1949. The books on the desk include a commemorative volume on the Laying of the Foundation Stone of the new House of Commons in 1948, minutes about the use of Churchill's telegrams by official historians, and, not surprisingly in the study of one of the most respectful of parliamentarians, two volumes of *Hansard*. Flanked by engravings after Kneller of the 1st Duke and Duchess of Marlborough hangs a full-length oil-portrait of Lady Churchill by Sir John Lavery, R.A. (1856–1941) inscribed to 'Mr Winston Churchill' and painted in 1915–16, while Churchill was at the Front. Beyond hangs a charcoal head and shoulders of Lady Randolph, Churchill's mother, by John Sargent. On the window-sill is a bronze horse and foal by Herbert Hazeltine.

The wall above the fireplace (which contains a seventeenth-century wrought iron fireback depicting the Annunciation) is dominated by an oil painting of Blenheim Palace, built by Vanbrugh for Churchill's great ancestor. Here, on November 30th 1874, when his parents were staying with his grandfather, the 7th Duke of Marlborough, Churchill was born prematurely in a small room on the ground floor. In January 1965 he was buried near by in the cemetery at Bladon, where he lies with his Churchill ancestors. The eighteenth-century view of Blenheim is by an unknown artist and shows the Palace across the lake from Rosamund's Well with Vanburgh's monumental bridge.

To the left and below hangs a painting which meant much to Churchill. It is by Edwin Ward and depicts his talented father, Lord

Randolph (1849–95), writing at his desk with a quill pen. Though Churchill never achieved intimacy with his Victorian father – he once told his own son Randolph when at Eton, 'I have talked to you more this holiday than my father talked to me in his whole life' – he admired him intensely, studied everything he wrote, and in 1906 at the age of thirty-two published his father's authoritative biography. It provided rich and tragic material. Lord Randolph, like his son, did not know the meaning of compromise. A resolute Tory, but with conceptions of Toryism incomprehensible to Tory back-benchers, he resigned in 1886 (on the issue of defence expenditure which seemed to him a matter of principle) the Chancellorship of the Exchequer and the leadership of the Tory party in the House of Commons. As his son was to do on more than one occasion, he went into political eclipse. Unlike his son, he never regained office, dying eight years later. Churchill had the Roman virtue of filial piety. He was determined not only in his biography to justify his father's career, but in his own political life to redeem his tragedy. It is both moving and suitable that the black despatch box, which he himself used when Chancellor of the Exchequer over forty years after his father relinquished the office, stands on the table under the portrait of Lord Randolph.

Beside the fireplace hang two small chalk drawings of her father by Sarah Churchill, and signed photographs of King George VI at Malta in June 1943 and of Roosevelt. Churchill and Roosevelt first met in Newfoundland in 1941 and subsequently on nine other occasions. Their mutual regard developed, in Churchill's words, into 'a dear and cherished friendship'. On the President's death in April 1945 Churchill was deeply moved, referring to him in parliament 'as the greatest champion of freedom who has ever brought help and comfort from the New World to the Old'.

The Study carpet is a Khorassan and was given to Churchill in Teheran in 1943 on his sixty-ninth birthday by the Shah of Persia. Three flags hang from the rafters: the union jack over the fireplace, hoisted in Rome on the night of June 5th 1944, was the first British flag to fly in a liberated capital, and was the gift of Field-Marshal Alexander; a replica of Churchill's standard as a Knight of the Garter; and his standard as Lord Warden of the Cinque Ports. The last was flown at Chartwell as Churchill's house-flag.

By the door stands a leather-covered chest, bearing the cypher of

Queen Anne. Though acquired by Lady Churchill, it is the type of ambassadorial chest that might well have been used by the 1st Duke of Marlborough. On the shelf above are personal photographs including one of the much-loved Nanny Everest.

THE STAIRS

On the floor outside the Study, the bronze lion is a representation of the lion of Luxembourg by the sculptor Tremont, and was a gift to Churchill with the freedom of the principality. The etching on the wall by Walter M. Keesey, inscribed to Churchill in 1920, is of unusual interest. It represents the first tank used in the battle of the Somme in 1916 and recalls Churchill's pioneer role in the development of mobile armour. Early in the war Churchill realised the need for a vehicle that could overrun trenches, and at his insistence a rudimentary tank was built and tested in May 1915. It was rejected, but again on Churchill's initiative another model was produced which at a crucial demonstration at Hatfield Park early in February 1916 won Lord Kitchener's approval. In September of the same year thirty-two tanks made their dramatic appearance on the Somme. In his conception of tank warfare, as in much else, Churchill was ahead of his time.

On the stairs hang three Churchill oils (Nos. 196, 395, 398). Facing the bottom of the stairs is a striking half-length portrait of Churchill by his friend Sir John Lavery, R.A. (1856–1941). He is in service uniform, wearing a French *poilu*'s tin-hat as he sometimes did when commanding the 6th Battalion of the Royal Scots Fusiliers in Flanders in 1916. The tin-hat hangs below the painting. The latter was presented by the officers of the Armoured Car Squadrons. No one, as we have seen, realised better than Churchill the importance of mobile armour or did more to further its development in the First World War.

On the second flight of stairs leading down to the Dining Room hang two more of Churchill's oils (Nos. 341 and 473) and a sketch of Randolph Churchill painted by John Lavery at Chartwell in 1932 and inscribed to Lady Churchill. In the small lobby on the stairs are exhibited several pages of the typescript of the concluding paragraphs of Volume III, Chapter XI, of *The World Crisis* with Churchill's manuscript corrections.

PORTRAIT OF LORD RANDOLPH AND DESPATCH BOX
Courtesy of British Travel Association

The steep slope of the land at Chartwell enabled Philip Tilden to situate his new Dining Room a flight below the Entrance Hall and yet at ground level. It was part of his scheme that the Dining Room, with its door on the lawn and its seven generous round-headed windows, should convey a sense of being almost part of the garden on which it looks.

In Churchill's later years the Dining Room was converted to a cinema, and a regular Sunday night film-show was held attended by family, guests, and staff. Films were sent down from London and in ordering them he no doubt sometimes took the advice of his friend Sir Alexander Korda. The room has now been put back exactly as it was before the war, and as it appears in William Nicholson's attractive canvas on the right-hand wall which shows the Churchills at the breakfast table in the early thirties. The painting was commissioned by friends to celebrate their silver wedding in 1933.

White walls, green curtains, glazed chintz, unstained oak, and rush matting create an effect of extreme simplicity. Yet much thought was given to the furniture. The dining and breakfast tables of plain seventeenth-century design were commissioned by the Churchills, as were the chairs, about which he had decided ideas. With his usual attention to detail he wrote a memorandum about them:

> The Dining Room chair has certain very marked requisites. First, it should be comfortable and give support to the body when sitting up straight; it should certainly have arms, which are an enormous comfort when sitting at meals. Second, it should be compact. One does not want the Dining Room chair spreading itself, or its legs, or its arms, as if it were a plant, but an essentially upright structure with the arms and the back almost perpendicularly over the legs. This enables the chairs to be put close together if need be, which is often more sociable, while at the same time the arms prevent undue crowding and elbowing.

Churchill got, as he usually did, precisely what he wanted. The chairs in the Dining Room conform to his specifications.

The dining table is set for tea and Sarah Churchill has described the pleasant teas at Chartwell with 'tomato-and-cucumber sandwiches and Gentleman's Relish for the gentlemen'. Yet tea was not a meal that Churchill himself regularly took or liked. The true associations of the Dining Room are with the talk that was the memorable feature of so many luncheons and dinners. They were rarely large or formal gatherings – the size of the house, particularly in the years when the children were growing up, excluded the possibility of large heterogeneous week-end parties – but the chosen guests heard unrivalled conversation. Churchill's imaginative and often provocative mind ranged over limitless territory, and his wonderful sense of phrase created an unforgettable impression on those who listened. Sometimes, when those masters of talk – Lloyd George, Birkenhead, Duff Cooper, and Beaverbrook – were at the table, the company made a contribution hardly less remarkable. In this century few rooms in England witnessed such conversation.

Meals, like everything else at Chartwell, were the product of Lady Churchill's flawless efficiency. Few husbands have had a house run with such competence. In the life of so unusual a man, details which in another context would be unworthy of mention acquire significance. Churchill preferred simple food, such things as an unsauced whiting with its tail in its mouth and a fine sirloin of beef, followed by a plain ice and a ripe Stilton. Champagne was usually served through dinner, which was at eight, and Pol Roger, the firm with which his friend Madame Pol Roger was associated, was among his favourite brands. 'A single glass of champagne', he said as a young man, 'imparts a feeling of exhilaration. The nerves are braced; the imagination is equally stirred; the wits become more nimble. A bottle produces a contrary effect.'

In the Dining Room on a table to the left of the fireplace – the latter contains a seventeenth-century Sussex fireback depicting St George and a lion rampant – lies the 'Golden Rose Book', an elephant folio bound in vellum given to Sir Winston and Lady Churchill in 1958 for their golden wedding by their children. It contains water-colours by many of the outstanding painters of the time – Augustus John, Duncan Grant, Ivor Hitchens, Matthew Smith, John Nash and others – illustrating twenty-nine of the thirty-two yellow and gold species, also their children's gift, planted in the Golden Rose Garden to commemorate the anniversary. The book marker was the gift of Sir George Bellew, Garter King of Arms.

On the oak table in the centre of the room is a crystal vase presented to Churchill in 1955 when he received the freedom of the borough of Harrow. As a schoolboy at Harrow he had successfully resisted conventional instruction and acquired a lasting love of the English language. He retained a great affection for the school and throughout his life continued to pay visits on Speech Day.

Below the painting by William Nicholson stands an impressive punch-bowl bearing the Copenhagen mark, which was given to Churchill by a group of admirers in Denmark. It is dedicated in Danish to Commodore Olbert Fischer, who commanded the Danish squadron at the battle of Copenhagen on April 2nd 1801, and the frieze in grisaille represents incidents in the engagement. It is one of twenty-five such bowls made in 1805–7. Only a dozen have survived. Nearby is a pile of cigar boxes. The brands are Romeo y Julieta and Camacho, the latter in boxes especially stamped for Churchill's use. He acquired a taste for good cigars when in Cuba as a war correspondent during the campaign of 1895, and his cigar subsequently became part of his public image. In later years he smoked up to ten cigars a day. However, he rarely got through more than half a cigar, and the butts were carefully kept for one of the gardeners, who was robust enough to savour Havana tobacco in a pipe.

Apart from the William Nicholson, the other paintings in this room are by Churchill (Nos. 172, 177, 371, 388, 391, 411). The painting over the oak side-table between the doors Churchill called a 'bottlescape' (No. 177), and it shows one of the Italian dwarf altar-candlesticks which have always stood on this side-table. Churchill to the distress of puritans enjoyed, as he enjoyed cigars, the good things that come in bottles, good wine and good brandy. He appreciated that they stimulated thought and conversation and were the natural friend of man. But he knew how to use them; they were his servants, not his master. The glass of whisky that was brought to him as he worked in the morning, and which he slowly sipped, was drowned to the brim in water and might well last until luncheon. His tastes in this matter were shared by such eminent predecessors as Walpole, the younger Pitt, Fox and Palmerston.

Below the 'bottlescape' stands a Japanese lacquer box inlaid with mother of pearl. It was a present on Churchill's ninetieth birthday from Shigeru Yoshida, Prime Minister of Japan from 1946 to 1947 and from 1948 to 1954.

5. *The Garden*

THE charm of the Garden relates to its simplicity. The plants are unpretentious. Such things as potentillas, fuchsias, and lavender predominate. The horticultural flavour is that of any pleasant country garden. The difference lies in the taste and skill of the planting and the lay-out. They are the expression of careful thought and affection and were Lady Churchill's preoccupation. She preferred, and achieved, simple and direct effects, and her love of cool colour found expression in massed white geraniums, white tulips, and cherry pie. The Garden also owes much to Mr. Vincent, who for nearly twenty years was Lady Churchill's head gardener and now under the National Trust ensures that the Garden preserves its special character.*

Emerging from the house a visitor sees below him a long terrace-lawn and the Chartwell woods rising to the skyline beyond. To the left across a smaller lawn lies a walled rose-garden, like so much else Lady Churchill's creation. Here, beside the steps, is a good specimen of *hydrangea villosa*. A herbaceous border provides a frame to the roses and four attractively trained standard wistaria.

From the rose-garden a path leads to a vine-covered loggia which terminates in the Marlborough Pavilion. The pavilion, built by Philip Tilden in the twenties, was Lady Churchill's idea and initially did not altogether commend itself to Churchill, who said, 'For my part I should have thought that one garden house, ten feet square, would accommodate all the sun that is our portion in English summers.' As an inscribed medallion on the ceiling records, the pavilion was decorated by John Spencer Churchill (Churchill's nephew) in 1949 as a birthday present from Lady Churchill.

On the north wall are the 1st Duke of Marlborough's arms and the

*The vast number of visitors has inevitably entailed certain changes, such as the paving of the paths which were originally grass.

family's Spanish motto, *Fiel Pero Desdichado* (Faithful but Unfortunate). The 1st Duke's father, a suffering and faithful royalist, obtained at the Restoration the right to augment his arms with the St George's Cross that appears in the first quarter. Marlborough's honours and fortune went through a daughter to the Spencer family, but in 1817 the 5th Duke added the name of Churchill to that of Spencer by royal licence, thus keeping in the family the surname of his great ancestor. Though in recent generations members of the family have tended to drop the Spencer prefix, the arms since 1817 have been quartered Spencer and Churchill and have been surmounted by two crests, the Churchill lion and the Spencer griffin's head.

Four terra-cotta plaques on the walls represent rivers associated with Marlborough's campaigns in the war of the Spanish Succession: the Danube, the Rhine with the siren of the Lorelei, the Meuse, and the Moselle with its famous vineyards. The canted corners of the pavilion contain terra-cotta medallions of John, Duke of Marlborough; his wife Sarah; Queen Anne who played so large a role in Marlborough's history and whose close favour Sarah enjoyed until replaced by her relative, Mrs Masham; and Prince Eugene of Savoy. The last (1663–1736) was the greatest Continental soldier of his generation and devoted his life to the service of the Holy Roman Empire. He first joined forces with Marlborough at Blenheim, and the close partnership that followed is perhaps unique in military history. A frieze in low relief round the ceiling evokes Marlborough's wars and one panel shows the defence of the village of Blenheim in 1704, prelude to the greatest of his victories.

From the pavilion the long terraced lawn, its line broken by one or two old yews, stretches below the house. *Hydrangea petiolaria* clothes part of the projecting wing and there is a good *magnolia grandiflora* on the south front, which Churchill particularly cherished. He loved painting the white waxen flowers which he could lean and pick from his bedroom window. From the lawn the unusual height of the building, dictated by the falling ground, is apparent.

At the far end of the terrace, where there is a chestnut of cyclopean proportions, flagged steps climb to a path that runs beside the highest of the many yew hedges at Chartwell. On the bank that borders the path are several buddleias. They meant much to Churchill, who loved butterflies. Lady Churchill planted them to attract, as they always do, particularly in late summer, brimstones, tortoiseshells, red admirals, and peacocks. Deploring the decrease of butterflies with the coming of artificial fertilisers, Churchill rather hoped that part of the fund raised by appeal in his eightieth year might have been used for their propagation. He also expressed the hope that after his death the National Trust would continue to foster at Chartwell the special plants that they love. The Trust is doing so.

Soon the path and the yew hedge take a right-angle turn to reveal a lawn. This was originally a grass tennis court. Lady Churchill was at one time a good player, and tennis a feature of Chartwell life. The court was converted to a croquet lawn after the war. Though Churchill sometimes took part in a game, swinging his mallet single-handed like a polo stick, Lady Churchill was the croquet expert and often played with her family and friends. Among the friends who joined in was Field-Marshal Montgomery, whose performance has been described as 'long on strategy, rather shorter on accurate play'.

Beyond the croquet lawn, two flagstones on the path mark the graves of Churchill's brown poodles. Rufus I was a thoroughly satisfactory dog and Churchill was much distressed when in 1947 he was run over at Brighton during the Conservative Party Conference. Rufus II, by all accounts a less-endearing animal, inspired none the less his master's extreme devotion.

Churchill had a love of animals and was able to gain their confidence. A robin at Chartwell fed from his hand and one of the Canada geese would leave the lake when he appeared and solemnly accompany him on his walks round the garden. Among his pets at Chartwell at various times were a badger, a young fox, and, in spite of the protests of his family, a malodorous sheep. There were also a succession of cats, a certain marmalade cat acquiring the distinction of being drawn by William Nicholson.

Beyond a high brick wall the path leads to a further terrace-lawn with seats overlooking the Weald. Below lies the Golden Rose Garden. The rose walk flanked by beech hedges, from which this part of the Garden takes its name, was created in 1958. It was the imaginative present which their children gave the Churchills on their golden wedding, and a tablet engraved by Reynolds Stone, set in the east wall, records the gift. Thirty-two yellow and gold rose species were planted in the two borders which run down the hill. In the centre of the rose walk stands a sundial. Its plinth is inscribed with the words 'Here lies the Bali dove'. Given to Lady Churchill in 1936 when she visited Bali on Lord Moyne's yacht (during the war he was to become Secretary of State for the Colonies, and then Deputy-Secretary of State in the Middle East, where he was assassinated by Jewish terrorists in 1944), the dove lived happily for two years at Chartwell. Round the plinth is engraved a quotation that recalls the dove's native island:

> 'It does not do to wander
> Too far from sober men,
> But there's an island yonder,
> I think of it again.'

The quotation, which comes from a poem by W. P. Ker, was suggested to Lady Churchill by Freya Stark.

This whole area, originally the kitchen garden, was the scene of Churchill's major activity as a brick-layer.* A limestone tablet in the east wall records that 'The greater part of this wall was built between the years 1925 and 1932 by Winston with his own hands'. He also built for his youngest daughter the little summer-house in the south-east corner. On the invitation of the General Secretary, Churchill in 1928 took out a card as an adult apprentice in the Amalgamated Union of Building Trade Workers. He was undoubtedly qualified to do so. The ensuing rumpus, and the angry resolutions passed, reflect the acerbated state of labour relations in the years immediately after the General Strike.

Through an archway in the bottom corner of the Golden Rose Garden, a flagged path, flanked on one side by Solomon's seal and lily of the valley, leads into an orchard. The inscribed oak bench beside the path was presented to Churchill on his eightieth birthday by the Epping Conservative Association. He represented the constituency for twenty-one years. When safely returned for the seat in 1924 he had unsuccessfully contested three elections in two years. Hence his observation, 'I have now found a resting place amid the glades of Essex.' On the right stands a group of tile-hung buildings with mellow red roofs. The first is Orchard Cottage built by Churchill specifically as a possible war-time retreat. The corner building was Churchill's Studio.

*To save labour the kitchen-garden was grassed down in 1966 and the present planting was carried out under the direction of Mr Lanning Roper.

6. *The Studio*

CHURCHILL left the Admiralty in May 1915 with the shadow of failure and the Dardanelles on his mind and on his reputation. It was at this time that experiments with a child's paint-box, and the encouragement of John Lavery and his talented wife, set him off and he began to paint. It was a solace and a resource, and remained so for the rest of his life. He once said, 'If it weren't for painting I couldn't live; I couldn't bear the strain of things.' Often in times of crisis or illness – when out of parliament in 1922, or later recuperating in the south of France – he found in painting a refreshment that enabled him to go back to work with clear judgement and renewed determination. In August 1945 after his rejection by the electorate, it was to painting that he naturally turned. Later he was to find in his canvases a screen from 'the envious eyes of Time and the surly advance of decrepitude'. In the trial of old age 'his beloved Muse . . . kept him company almost to the end'.

If painting was a solace to Churchill, it was also and always an intense pleasure. He relished colour, canvas, and the problems they presented and he set about the solution of these problems with delight and gusto. It is impossible to read his essay on *Painting as a Pastime* without being fired to emulate him. His attitude to painting, as this perceptive essay reveals, was direct and unpretentious: 'Go out into the sunlight and be happy with what you see.' It reads refreshingly in a period when polysyllabic mystagogues pontificate about the craft he practised.

Churchill was fortunate in that the two most distinguished artists of his day, Walter Sickert and William Nicholson, were personal friends who came to stay and paint at Chartwell. Sickert in a fortnight, Churchill said, imparted 'his considered wisdom' and Nicholson, who was a visitor for longer periods, taught him even more. His first steps in painting, however, were learnt from two other friends, John Lavery and William Orpen, both talented portrait painters. It was Orpen, realising Churchill's response to colour, who first advised him to paint in Provence. His formative painting lesson was given by Lady Lavery. One day as he gingerly confronted the snow-white expanse of his first canvas, he heard a car draw up. As he delightfully recounts:

> From this chariot there stepped swiftly and lightly none other than the gifted wife of Sir John Lavery. 'Painting! But what are you hesitating about? Let me have a brush – the big one.' Splash into the turpentine, wallop into the blue and white, frantic flourish on the palette – clean no longer – and then several large fierce strokes and slashes of blue on the absolutely cowering canvas. Anyone could see that it would not hit back. No evil fate avenged the jaunty violence. The canvas grinned in helplessness before me. The spell was broken. The sickly inhibitions rolled away. I seized the largest brush and fell upon my victim with Berserk fury. I have never felt any awe of a canvas since.

Audacity, attack, feeling for a broad brush and love of colour, were to characterise his work. He admitted that Sickert did not find him an apt pupil for he rejoiced in highlights and bright colours. He was 'genuinely sorry for the poor browns' which Sickert laid under such splendid tribute.

Though several portraits are exhibited in the Studio, Churchill was primarily a landscape and still-life painter. He had always responded immediately and perceptively to landscape and he discovered, as most painters do, that his craft sharpened and intensified his responses. Painting brought him closer to the country and enabled him to see into it more deeply. His work, as Sir John Rothenstein has said, essentially reflects 'sheer joy in the simple beauties of nature; water, still, bubbling, or agitated by wind; snow immaculate and crisp; trees dark with the density of their foliage or dappled by sunlight; fresh flowers; distant mountains, and, above all, sunlight at its fiercest.' It is surely not mere chance that men and events, with which nine-tenths of his life were passionately concerned, should be rigorously excluded from his work. It was to gain respite from their pressures, to establish contact with a world unrelated to elections, manoeuvres, and the pre-occupations of the body politic, that Churchill repeatedly set up his easel. From this world, enriched and fortified, he returned to the combat.

Though he made no claims for his paintings, some of Churchill's landscapes are more than competent. If he learnt his craft in middle age, he certainly cultivated – again to quote Sir John Rothenstein – 'the possibilities open to him with assiduity and resource'. None the less, the chief interest of his work lies in its relation to his life, a life whose course influenced every Englishman of two generations. 'Do not turn', he said in a somewhat different context, 'the critical eye of passivity upon these efforts.' The appeal is justified. The essential question is whether Churchill would have been the same man, and achieved as much, without the comfort and delight which he found in painting. There can be only one answer.

Churchill first exhibited under the pseudonym of 'Charles Morin' and paintings so signed must be extremely rare. Later increasing confidence prompted him to send a canvas to the Royal Academy (1947). It was the first of twenty-four pictures hung at Summer Exhibitions, and in 1948 he was elected Honorary Academician Extraordinary.

Churchill's easel with an unfinished canvas stands in the large recess in the Studio and a generous supply of paint in capacious tubes is set beside it. The armchair in which he painted was bequeathed him by Sir Ian Hamilton. The unfinished head on the stand beside the easel, Churchill's first and only essay as a sculptor, represents Oscar Nemon. While the latter was executing a bust of the statesman, Churchill returned the compliment and modelled the sculptor. It is said to be a remarkable likeness. The walls are hung with a number of unframed canvases in various stages of completion.

Over the Studio door is the head of a *tauro bravo*, killed on V.E. day by one of the greatest matadors of all time. It bore a white 'V' on its forehead, and the inscription below it reads:

> This bull 'Perdigon', which came from my stud, was fought at Valencia by Manolete on the day of Victory. It was most noble in its ferocity and was born with the sign of victory on its brow.
>   I present it to the great Mr Winston Churchill, who with exemplary valour, nobility and humanity, wrought the victory which will save the world.
>
>   José Escobar.

The bust of Rudyard Kipling in front of the window, given to Churchill on his eightieth birthday, also bears a significant inscription. It reads 'One sang of Empire and the other saved it.'

The large modern tapestry once hung in the Belgian parliament. Churchill admired it when he went to Brussels to receive the freedom of the city and it was afterwards given to him. Against it stand a white marble bust of Lady Randolph Churchill, an old leather armchair, and a damaged portrait of Lord Randolph. Churchill has described how once when copying this portrait he clearly saw his father sitting in the leather chair near by and how they embarked on a long discussion of men and events, and of the changes which had overtaken the world in more than half a century.

The mammoth globe beside the large window, one of two globes specially made for Roosevelt and Churchill so that they might the more easily assess the fortunes of a world at war, was the gift of the United States War Department.

On the oak table at the far end of the Studio is an admirably executed model of a naval gun made and presented in 1918 by the workers of the Ponders End Shell Works. Beside it are the Sten gun issued to Churchill for his protection in the Second World War, and his tin helmet. To the left of the table are a bundle of the polo sticks which he used to such good effect, and to the right a further selection of his many walking-sticks.

The paintings in the main body of the Studio represent a further selection of Churchill's works. A large canvas by a Russian painter, more notable for historic than artistic interest, portrays Churchill, Roosevelt, and Stalin at Yalta. A table on the right carries a number of mementos, among them Churchill's wartime passport, his ration book, and identity card.

Appendix I

CHURCHILL PAINTINGS IN THE HOUSE AT CHARTWELL
Grateful acknowledgement is made to the catalogue of Churchill's paintings compiled by David Coombs (*Churchill His Paintings*, Hamish Hamilton, 1967). The numbers assigned to the pictures at Chartwell are those in the Coombs catalogue.

Apart from experiment with tempera after the Second World War, Churchill painted almost exclusively in oils and on canvas or hardboard, though a few paintings exist on panel. He obtained his effects by colour rather than draughtsmanship. Sometimes, following a close preliminary study of his subject, he painted with great rapidity (see No. 391); on other occasions he carefully worked up a detailed subject in the studio from photographs, even making use, as many distinguished painters have done, of an image projected on his canvas from a magic lantern or a photographic slide. His paintings, when signed, are most usually inscribed with the initials 'WSC'.

It is significant of the fact that Churchill's painting was primarily the 'product of a man off duty', a relaxation in times of adversity, and a record of home life, holiday, and travel, that only three of the paintings in the house were executed when Churchill was in office (Nos. 6, 96 and 473).

4 *Plug Street*, 1916.
Churchill had begun to paint in the previous year. The title is a familiar corruption of Ploegstraat, Churchill's regimental headquarters when in command of the 6th Battalion of the Royal Scots Fusiliers in the First World War.

6 *Roses, c.* 1928.

7 *Mallows, c.* 1928.

68 *Trees by a Stream in Norfolk, c.* 1923.
Churchill painted many Norfolk landscapes when staying at

Breccles Hall with Edwin Montagu (1879–1924), whose brilliant wife, Venetia Stanley, was Lady Churchill's cousin. Montagu was Secretary of State for India from 1917 to 1922.

The Atlas Mountains appear in the distance. Churchill painted in Morocco over a span of more than twenty years.

THE STUDIO

Courtesy of G. P. King

Churchill painted several pictures at Hever Castle, Lord Astor's house near Chartwell.